UNTOLD MAFIA TALES FROM THE FBI TOP HOODLUM SQUAD:

The Storied Legacy of FBI Special Agent, Peter C. Clemente and His Ground Zero Organized Crime Battle with the American Mafia

BOOK ONE
CARLO GAMBINO, BOSS OF BOSSES

by:

Peter C. Clemente
&
G.P. Clemente

Digital design by:
TELEMACHUS PRESS

This book is a work of non-fiction. The basic facts of the events and characters are reportedly true. The details presented here have been filtered through the authors' memories. Some of the names have been changed, or not used, to protect personal identities.

UNTOLD MAFIA TALES FROM THE FBI TOP HOODLUM SQUAD:
The Storied Legacy of FBI Special Agent, Peter C. Clemente and His Ground Zero Organized Crime Battle with the American Mafia
Book One: Carlo Gambino, Boss Of Bosses
Copyright © 2024 All rights reserved, including the right to reproduce this book, or portions thereof, in any form. No part of this text may be reproduced, transmitted, downloaded, decompiled, reverse engineered, or stored in or introduced into any information storage and retrieval system, in any form or by any means, whether electronic or mechanical without the express written permission of the author. The scanning, uploading, and distribution of this book via the Internet or via any other means without the permission of the publisher is illegal and punishable by law. Please purchase only authorized electronic editions and do not participate in or encourage electronic piracy of copyrighted materials.

Copyright registration number: TXu 2–437-348
Effective July 27, 2024

The publisher does not have any control over and does not assume any responsibility for author or third-party websites or their content.

Cover designed by G. P. Clemente

Published by G. P. Clemente

ISBN: 979-8-218-47781-3 (paperback)

Version 2024.09.19

Dedication

Dedicated to my beloved Bea, who watched over me
from the highest perch possible while crafting this,
and of course, my father, alongside her,
who left behind these riches of his life for all to ponder.

Contents

Forward i
Chapter 1: The Golden Gates of Hell 1
Chapter 2: Mob Rule 7
Chapter 3: Spy v. Spy 12
Chapter 4: Tommy Palmer, Lion in Decline 23
Chapter 5: The Summit of Mount Apalachin 27
Chapter 6: Boss of Bosses, Destroyer of Worlds 31
Chapter 7: Moment of Judgement 38
About the Authors 45

Forward

Much of this was written directly and handed down, not just to me, but to those who desire a record of the events that transpired during the Mafia's "golden years" from the early 1950s until the late 80s. My father, Peter C. Clemente, throughout my entire life around him, told me not only stories of knights and kings and dragons being slayed as a boy, but also of fire breathing creatures who ruled the land with a roundtable of characters loyal only to a ruthless king. They were the "Men of Honor," they called themselves, and as I got older, I understood better why he left us every morning to do battle with these dangerous warriors who were far from being respectable or romantic.

When I was finally old enough to make sense of what La Cosa Nostra or "Our Thing" in more sinister Italian terms meant, the real meaning and importance of my father's work took hold. I remember one day feeling the gravity of how fearsome this "Mafia" had become while looking at a picture for the first time of Albert "the Mad Hatter" Anastasia's bullet filled body, covered with blood-soaked towels at the floor of a barber chair. It gave me concern about the vulnerability of America and how brutal these short, squat, but deadly Italian American gangsters had shown themselves to be in their obsessive climb to power. They became no longer the fairy tale figures my father conjured as a boy in my innocence. The characters in the legend now pillaged not villages, but United States coffers to the tune of billions of dollars; stormed not castles, but the government buildings of corrupted judges, politicians and police officials; and slayed not just each other in bloody carnage, but sometimes the innocent if they dared get in their way, willfully or not.

Born in 1922 in Brooklyn, New York, the offspring of Sicilian immigrants, the years to come would produce a storied life for the son of Salvatore and Emily Clemente. One that germinated during the Depression years, and later in World War II as an Army surgical tech in war torn Philippines before a G. I. Bill law degree from St. Johns University allowed him to proudly hang his shingle as an attorney in the Big Apple. Soon after, when meeting the love of his life, my mother, Theresa nee Cerro, their embrace bonded not just each other, but their birthright as part of the Greatest Generation.

Before his passing in 2017, just short of his 95th birthday, my father left behind a treasure cache of documents he authored and amassed during the course of his 26-year FBI career from 1950-1976 and following his retirement. His ascension to the FBI's elite Top Hoodlum Squad in 1957, following the infamous Apalachin crime summit came at the pinnacle of his career. His tap on the shoulder by J. Edgar Hoover to become one of the rare Sicilian speaking agents did not deter the revulsion and shame these fellow Italian and Sicilian American hoodlums had brought to him and his people, however glitzy and monetarily seductive they had become.

This is not only my father's story, but his recording of historical events that would evolve over the years from darkened clouds metastasizing in the shadows of evil to rays of abundant sunshine. Thanks to his efforts and that of the dedicated FBI agents that worked alongside him to rid the world of the Mafia's stranglehold, they were truly unrecognized American heroes. Save some minor editing, these are just some of his stories passed down verbatim about his historic encounter in 1962 with the world's most powerful Mafia king, Carlo Gambino—his first ever face to face encounter with him and then later during an electronic surveillance of Gambino at the Golden Gate Motel in Miami Beach. The story weaves other tales and perspectives along the way and the adventure we are guided through shows more than aptly how the human condition on both sides of law is somehow similar in nature. It is told in a way few others could have articulated these events, with keen insight, reflection, common sense and more than its share of riveting tension and comic relief. Hopefully, through this, the legacy of a true American hero will live on.

        This one's for you, Pop. God bless.
              —*G. P. (Gary) Clemente*

UNTOLD MAFIA TALES FROM THE FBI TOP HOODLUM SQUAD:

The Storied Legacy of FBI Special Agent, Peter C. Clemente and His Ground Zero Organized Crime Battle with the American Mafia

BOOK ONE
CARLO GAMBINO, BOSS OF BOSSES

Chapter One
The Golden Gates of Hell
"How many tanks and planes do you have to go against the FBI?"

The daily boredom of listening for the return of the man in the next room suddenly evaporated. In between long periods of his absence, I either dozed off or entertained myself with the Miami Herald crossword puzzle. My partner, Frank Doerner, who was stretched out on the couch catching a few ZZ's, heard the string of profanities I blurted unexpectedly.

Frank swung his long legs around to the floor and sat up. He looked at me anxiously and asked, "What's up, Pete? "

I listened a few more seconds through the headphones to make certain I was hearing what I thought I heard. I had picked up the sound of a key turning in the lock and then a conversation that electrified me more than the others we had caught on tape.

"Son of a bitch," I said, "Carlo, Vincent and Tommy are back in the room, talking Sidge (Sicilian), cursing the FBI and making a big ruckus."

I was picking up muffled, excited male voices in the hallway, just outside of Carlo's motel suite. That was unusual for Carlo, who made a practice of not talking in the hallway. The Carlo that Frank and I were eavesdropping on was Carlo Gambino, head of the most powerful of the five New York crime families of La Cosa Nostra (LCN), meaning "Our

Thing," in Italian, the American equivalent of the Mafia. As the crime boss of several hundred career criminals, killers and sociopaths, he was the most powerful criminal in the world, never mind the United States. A millionaire many times over, yet there he was staying in the upper middle class Golden Gate Motel in the suite next to ours. He could have afforded the posh Fontainebleau or the Eden Roc, but he desired anonymity, hence the attractive, but off the beaten path accommodation in Miami Beach.

I anticipated the usual busy day transcribing the revealing chats he had with his lieutenants, but something was amiss. The men with Gambino—Vincent "Jimmy Dee" Palmisano and Tommy Greco, aka Tommy Palmer, were spitting out curses in Sicilian and were super-hot. The curses were not run of the mill gutter profanity. Mixed in with the shop-worn four-letter words were calls upon heaven and hell to inflict all manner of calamities upon the FBI agents who had surveyed and photographed them for the first time during Carlo Gambino's six-week Florida winter vacation. Somebody must have given the brick agents the OK to give Gambino and his New York hoods the same ball buster treatment agent Ralph Hill always employed to rattle the cage of Sam "Momo" Giancana, the Chicago LCN boss. Hill and the Chicago agents drove Giancana to distraction, making it almost impossible for him to perform his duties as chieftain of the Chicago family.

Frank wriggled into his size-twelve shoes and asked if he could hear what was going on through the reel-to-reel tape recorder, so I handed him the headset. Frank put one earpiece to his ear and listened a while.

"Sounds like your paisanos are having a blowout. The only English I can hear is 'those bastards...the FBI...those pricks.' Six weeks without mention of us, why now?"

He handed the set back to me and headed for the couch. "Well, obviously," I said, "the only thing that's changed on the radar is the agents on the street screwed things up big time. Why in hell, when they know we're busting our hump here, would they even think of taking a chance in exposing us by tailing them, number one, and number two, not having the sense that God gives by being so obvious with taking pictures of them in plain sight?"

I could see how nervous Frank was getting. "Yeah, the cat's out of the bag. Now they know we know Carlo's in town. That's going to cause problems on the wire for us." The wire he was referring to were the tiny strategic microphones that were placed next door in Gambino's room inside the telephone A-blocks, a 2 by 2-inch phone wiring installation commonly fastened to the floor baseboards of every building during that era. The bugging mission was stealthily engineered one morning as quickly as possible by a team of sound technicians entering Gambino's room after Carlo and his wife Kate left the premises for a day out on the town.

The operation took place in March, 1962 and I knew plenty about Mr. Gambino even as far back as when I first accosted him face-to-face on the street for a historic meeting. I will never forget the piercing glare he gave me that was the look of a hawk. The pronounced beak of a nose accentuated his gaze and when it fell on you, no one could help the feeling of being sized up like smalls bit of prey, women and children included. Up to that point, I had been the first agent ever to write up an official government summary on Mr. Gambino following the notorious Apalachin mob conclave in upstate New York where he was arrested at the 53-acre estate of mobster Joe "the Barber" Barbara, on November 14, 1957. Gambino, through popular myth, was famously known on the streets as the Boss of Bosses (capo di tutti capi), but had never been officially given that designation by his peers or the mob Commission. The last such formal honoree was Salvatore Maranzano, in 1931 following his takeover of the New York rackets from Joe Masseria during the Castellammarese War. It was Maranzano who was instrumental in forming the Five Families in New York.

Gambino, through the years, would become the most powerful of that quintet, a breed of super criminal that could nonchalantly send men to their graves with just a nod of the head or even with one of those looks. To my mind though, this short, plain looking man's omnipotence was overrated in the grand scheme of things. Who among any of us, could not send others to their grave if we wanted to? Whether we drove our cars or school buses with precious cargo in them, commanded a troop of Boy Scouts in the wilderness or maybe stood watch over a helpless infant, the power of life and death rested with each of us. But Mr. Gambino, I was sure, had his own rational escape route from the killing and mayhem that lay at his feet. All the blame, guilt and eternal damnation from ending another man's life was easily washed from his hands with a simple order to have someone else pull the trigger for him. I was sure that he would have made a great character from Shakespeare, magnificent as a born leader of men, but too horribly flawed to redeem himself through introspection.

After I put the headphones back on, Frank asked me, "What are they talking about? They always switch to dialect when they're excited or have something important to say."

I signaled Frank to wait. "We're in deep shit, Frank. They're on to us. They're all talking at once because the agents outside poked the hornet's nest. Carlo's having another heart attack or has acid indigestion. It's bedlam. Tommy Palmer recommends turning on the radio. That's a bad sign, so they can mask their conversations when a bug is suspected."

The situation takes a turn for the worse when Palmer, senior in rank to Palmisano, tells Vincent to check on Don Carlo's condition, reminding him that the boss had open heart surgery and several heart attacks previously. I hear Vincent saying, "Do you think the FBI harassed the old man today hoping he would drop dead from a heart attack? Those FBI pricks will stop at nothing. They embarrassed Petey Pumps (Ferrara) by interviewing his daughter, who was a nun in a convent once."

I tell Frank I'm hearing that Don Carlo it seems, is having an attack of acid indigestion and not joining his two underlings in their vituperative attack on the FBI. "Vincent, be a good fella," he says, "go into the bedroom and bring me that drugstore bag on the counter. I need to take a nitro pill and some soda bicarb."

Vincent and Tommy, who were still angrily spinning out of control over being photographed and openly tailed right up to the door of the hotel, suddenly stop their yammering as they blurt out, "Holy shit, those f--king bastards, maybe you're having a heart attack? You want I should call a doctor?"

"No, I want you to *statu sittu* (be quiet)," says Gambino. "I shouldn't have had that appetizer at lunch, the fried calamari with creamed garlic sauce. I should listen to my wife and stay away from fried foods. Of course, having the FBI on our ass all afternoon didn't help my digestion."

A loud burp is heard, followed by Carlo's, "excuse me." I thought to myself, the fried squid and FBI hounding him could prove a deadly combination, similar to the lethal ice bullet in the Dick Tracy comics, and just as hard to recover as evidence.

Vincent tries to talk tough, probably to impress the old man. "Say the word, Don Carlo and I'll teach that prick Elmer Mullen, the guy with the camera a little lesson."

Obviously unruffled by the FBI's delicate and open confrontation, which has Tommy and Vincent breathing fire and brimstone, Gambino tells Vincent, "Stop talking nonsense. We don't lay a hand on the law. You want to start a war with the government? How many tanks and planes do you have to go against the FBI?"

Vincent has obviously handed over some of Gambino's medications. "Thanks. Give me one of the nitro pills. Tommy, stop talking to yourself. You're playing into their hands. Make yourself useful. Put two teaspoons of the bicarb in a glass of plain water and bring it to me." Momentarily, I'm guessing that Gambino has now swallowed some of it because I hear, "Christ, Tommy, you trying to kill me, I said two not four teaspoons."

"I did."

"Show me the spoon! I thought so. Tommy… my blessed mother, God rest her soul, told me the rocky road to hell is paved with good intentions."

"What do you mean, boss?"

"Tommy, that's a *tablespoon* you used, not a teaspoon. There's almost three teaspoons in a tablespoon. It was more like six teaspoons of bicarb in that glass of water. If you had put in a little more, a guy wouldn't have to be Jesus Christ to walk across that water." I smiled. At this point, I couldn't help thinking these blood thirsty hoods had now degenerated into the Three Stooges.

"I'm sorry boss, that business with the FBI has me steamed."

"Forget it, will ya. A friend of mine told me his mother-in-law, who couldn't speak or read English was visiting from the old country. One day, while my friend and his wife were out doing some shopping, the old lady takes it into her head to make a pizza for them. She takes down off the closet shelf a bag she thinks is white flour and adds the water and yeast to the center of a mound of what she thinks is flour. Her daughter and son-in-law come home to find her in tears, because she can't work the dough. My friend looks at the bag and discovers she was using by mistake, plaster of paris."

Listening to Carlo, I could understand why he had risen to the height of his power. He was distracting them with a story to bring them down from their highly excitable state. I heard Carlo belch and knew he was feeling better.

During the entire six weeks it was anything but glamorous espionage work like in James Bond. Mostly it was tedious, eight hours a day on my shift and eight more for Frank on his. Many times, it was longer for me because of the Italian being spoken that needed a quick translation and my partner didn't know how to handle it when he wore the headset. When Palmer or Tommy Luchese (aka, Three Finger Brown, from the loss of some digits) came by for late evening meetings or after Gambino and Kate had dinner with Luchese and his wife Kitty, I found myself pulling extra duty deciphering their conversations.

Chapter Two
Mob Rule
"They could be down the street or in the next room for all we know."

There were ample reasons why Carlo had ascended to power in the manner he did. A big one was his diabolical attention to detail. Like a calculating Chief Financial Officer who had his accountants spied on by other bean counters to prevent theft, Gambino left no stone unturned. Money, of course, was the root of all his evil, but he collected his tribute without a death wish. During the era of the Late Roman Empire, nearly 60% of its emperors were either executed or assassinated. It was no different for the empire's descendants in the modern-day Italian Mafia where King Henry's proclamation, "uneasy lies the head that wears a crown," was a fate to be reckoned. Always looking over his shoulder, no matter how lofty he was, Emperor Gambino always got his hands dirty by asking questions.

I heard Carlo return to Vincent's mention of agent Elmer Mullins and asked if it was possible that he had been followed to the motel. "How come you know this Elmer Mullins? Did he follow you here? I told you fellas I didn't want you bringing any heat on me. Everything's been okay up to now. All of a sudden, the FBI is swarming around us. What provoked that? Have you been mouthing off to this *sbirro* (police spy)? You know, Vincent you got to keep a civil tongue in your mouth even when they provoke you.

Ignore them. Act like you don't even know if they're there. I didn't like you calling them names. You piss them off and they'll dump on you."

Vincent gets defensive, whines, "No chance boss. Give me credit for common sense. I left my house this morning before it got late and went to the Rascal House for breakfast. No one was on the street. I made sure no one followed me here. I don't know how Mullins and his pack of hyenas got on us. He goes around town with that camera like the New York Daily News, taking photos of the boys. Is that so Tommy? He's tight with security at Hialeah and the other tracks. Every time I'm at the track picking up some bets, this cucumber shows up to bust my balls. The guy's a real hayseed from the sticks, but a first class *scutia menti* (ball buster)."

Tommy Palmer, which is the name Tommy Greco has been going by since he first started pushing tins of bootleg alcohol that Carlo and his brothers were producing in New Jersey, reluctantly agrees with Vincent.

TOMMY: I've seen that little baldheaded jerk at the track, huddling with the jockeys looking for tips. He's a two dollar better. Joe Farinella's brother, Nick, the guy whose family has that rundown looking motel on Biscayne Boulevard that the 'lamsters' use, one day at Hialeah, pointed him out to me as an FBI agent. I remember his face, but not his name. The *schemu* (moron) looks like a race track tout. He doesn't worry me, this is his territory, but what bugs me is what the hell is that Warren Donovan and his partner Pat McCarthy, both New York agents, doing in Miami?

At this point, Tommy drops his voice to almost a whisper and says, "Let's not say anything we don't want the sbirri (police spies) to hear. You know the walls may have ears. I smell a rat." Moments later, I hear the volume on the radio turned up.

CARLO: What do you mean rat? A stoolie?

TOMMY: I mean, I think the FBI in New York got word you were coming to Miami and told them here to expect you. That Donovan guy and his red-faced partner have been hassling the buttons (made men) in the family trying to turn them. Donovan tries to speak Italian and shows off how much he knows about family business—this guy, that guy, he says he's hooked up with Jigs Forlano, so on and so forth, you know what I mean? His pronunciation is bad, but I gotta give him credit. He knows what's going on in our *borgata* (family). What I am concerned with, after the bullshit they pulled on us today, following our ass everywhere we went, as well as that guy Mullen with this f--ing camera—it's not a stoolie I'm worried about, it's those bugs those bastards have been planting.

CARLO: I know about wiretaps. Back in 1930, the Treasury, Alcohol, Tobacco and Tax Unit put a wiretap on the phone we were using for business. They had us by the *palle* (balls) and the case was about to go to trial when the Supreme Court had a similar case to ours and ruled wiretaps were illegal. They dismissed the case against us. My lawyer tells me the FBI stretches the wiretap law. If they don't follow the guidelines, they can't use what they hear. It would be illegal for them to use it against us. Don't think for a minute Hoover likes us any better than the commies, do you? I'm telling you, we were an embarrassment to the FBI when we were caught with our pants down at Joe Barbara's place, thanks to that jackass Vito (Genovese). If you think that the FBI, put their eavesdropping equipment in mothballs like the Navy did some of their battleships, I have a bridge to sell you.

VINCENT: Those bastards could be eavesdropping on us right now. They could be down the street or in the next room for all we know.

TOMMY: One of the capos in New York has a friend of a friend who knows that guy Spindel, the private eye who's a whiz on bugs. He used him to get the goods on his wife, who was banging the pool cleaner. He said they can be on the other side of town. All they have to do is lease a telephone line and feed the info from the tap or the microphone onto the leased line. They don't have to be next-door.

CARLO: My lawyer tells me the telephone companies are in bed with the FBI.

At that point, I had not asked Frank to turn the recorder back on because I didn't want a recording made of some of the things done by the agents outside who were supposed to be maintaining a loose and discreet physical surveillance of Carlo so that he would feel relaxed and free of FBI scrutiny. Then again, the boys might have received the go-ahead order from the SAC (Special Agent in Charge) to do exactly what they did. Either way, it was making for some uncomfortable moments for us and for Frank Doerner in particular. Frank was at long last in his OP (office of preference). Like so many other FBI agents, his was the typical case in that he had spent much of his government career between undesirable metropolitan areas around the country with little hope of ever reaching his OP. In Frank's case, there was an additional sorry twist of fate.

While he was a supervisor at the SOG (Seat of Government) on the ladder to administrative advancement, he received both a letter of transfer to Indianapolis, Indiana and a letter of censure. One year into his Indiana exile, it became providential for him, but not his mother-in-law, whom he loved as his own mother, when she suffered a disabling disease. Drawing on his talents as a creative writer and his knowledge of the foibles of Director Hoover, Frank drafted a "hardship letter," requesting a transfer to Miami so as to care for his mother-in-law, which elicited the desired response after reaching the desk of Mr. Hoover. The Director respected dutiful sons who cared for aging parents as he had with his own mother until she died at an advanced old age.

Frank was granted his dream OP, the Miami office, and he had just arrived a month before when he was tapped for the Gambino monitoring job. His wife and family were still in Indianapolis, waiting on the sale of their home and the end of his children's school year. Frank spoke English uncommonly well, but he knew no Sicilian. Since Carlo was the subject of the eavesdropping and his associates restricted any discussions of Mafia matters to Sicilian, it was my temporary assignment with Frank to translate to Sicilian portions of the tapes. So it was, that Frank Doerner, freshly arrived at his OP, but not yet firmly established, was the one in the hot seat and stood to lose the most should anything go wrong while we snooped on the Boss of Bosses.

Chapter Three
Spy v. Spy
"Damn it. They're not trashing the room. They're looking for a bug."

Bernard F. Conners, writer extraordinaire and author for books, is also a former FBI agent (1951-1959) who penned *Don't Embarrass the Bureau*, where he gave his description of an OP. "The OP is truly a gift from the heavens. A gift to be cherished, revered, and protected. Reaching one's OP was one thing and staying there was something else again."

Agent Conners and I toiled in the mines of organized crime in New York as part of the Top Hoodlum Squad and he never abided the suffocating and restrictive efforts of the Director and his administrative staff of sycophants and hypocrites to mold him in Hoover's image. Despite the excitement of participating in the 1956 investigation of an acid attack that blinded nationally known labor columnist Victor Riesel and other high-profile cases, Conners left the Bureau to work for the Canada Dry corporation and then the world of literature where he went onto bigger and better things.

In short, a discovered bug by the Gambino crew next door could catapult Doerner out of his OP and onto the copper slag heaps of Butte, Montana or Broken Bow, Idaho. I called over to Frank to turn on the recorder because I sensed that things were building up again on the other side of the wall like the bulging magma dome in Mount Saint Helens before it horrifically blew out. There were ample grounds for anxiety on my partner's behalf that he deserved to be aware of. His fate rested in the hands of the organized crime gods. Frank reignited the tape recorder on the table I was at and I handed him the headset. Their conversations about eavesdropping by the FBI hadn't disturbed me one whit, but actually searching for a bug was an insect of another color.

They had not started the actual search until I handed Frank the headset. He listened with one earpiece and couldn't understand what they were saying so he did not realize his OP was in jeopardy. He handed the set back to me and headed for the couch. "No English at all coming through," he said. "Are all you goombahs so emotional? They sound like they're trashing the room. Maybe they're going to steal the furniture," he joked nervously.

I was a little miffed with Frank's goombah remark, so I told him that Carlo was a multimillionaire and could buy and sell us many times over.

I listened some more through the wire and became really alarmed.

Vincent and Tommy had kicked the conversation up about bugs and had worked themselves into a frenzy of suspicion again. Their expletives were flying everywhere, making their earlier profanities sound like the recitation of the rosary as they took the Lord's name in vain while calling the Holy Mother a whore. Hoover and the Miami agents came in for their fair share of vituperation, too. Tommy Palmer wished all the agents would get cancer and their private parts would rot and fall off. It was Tommy who got them so whipped up that they began looking for the bug in earnest. None of them had ever seen a miniature microphone in their lifetime, nor was it likely they would recognize what it was if they stumbled on it.

"Damn it." I told Frank, "They're not trashing the room, they're looking for a bug. The old man isn't saying much, but Vincent and Tommy are still cursing the FBI." This is not what Frank wanted to hear.

"Did you say they're looking for the bug? Tell me it isn't so." Frank reached for the headset and listened with an incredulous look on his face. "Crap, you're right." He threw the headset back to me as if it was burning his hand. "We need to pull the mic before they find it, Pete. My OP is riding on the outcome of this. My wife will leave me if I get transferred again. She doesn't know how the Bureau operates. It's bad enough she believes I may have done something terrible to get busted from supervisor to brick agent and be transferred to Indianapolis."

Our guys taking their pictures didn't put the idea in Tommy Palmer's mind that we might be bugging Carlos's room. What really gave him that thought was Tommy's recognition of Donovan and McCarthy as two agents from New York. Tommy figured our guys had not recently discovered Carlo's presence in Miami, that the agents must have followed him to Florida, therefore the Miami office knew in advance he was coming and where he was going, giving them enough time to bug his suite.

For a man who was facing another letter of censure, a looming transfer and abandonment by his wife, Frank was concerned, but tensely composed. I wasn't sure if he was trying to pry away a particle of food stuck in his molar or if he was developing a nervous tic. There were beads of perspiration that formed on his upper lip and hairline temple. Matter of fact, I wasn't any dryer. The comfortable Hawaiian shirt I wore was now sticking to my back and my underarms were wet.

Frank had been in the Bureau a few years more than me and was one GSA grade higher than me and could have used that seniority to force me to pull the microphone, but he didn't. Most likely he understood I could make a more reasoned decision because I digested better and faster what was going on next door. Still, he stood over the wire, tantalizingly close, waiting for me to agree with him to pull it.

Tommy Palmer's realization that the FBI was aware of Carlo's presence in Miami, coupled with their active search of the room for the suspected bug made me wish the monitoring site we occupied at the hotel was farther removed than the wall that separated us and Carlo's suite. The Miami FBI soundman, acting on short notice, had done the best he could given what he was forced to work with. Not all monitoring sites were as precariously placed as the one we were manning. Another agent, Eddie Dunn, told me that while he was assigned to the resident agency in Providence, Rhode Island, he monitored the bug in mobster Raymond Patriarca's vending machine business office from a secure room in a

Catholic convent no less. Eddie said he used to sit there in comfort, snacking on cookies and cakes the good Sisters baked each day for him, fresh and hot, while he listened to and recorded the sinful conversations of Patriarca, the boss of the New England family of La Cosa Nostra.

I came to learn that spying on others while in close quarters can lead to strange bedfellows. There was an agent named Jim Hill who was the FBI's Supervisor of Sound during the years before and after the famous Apalachin mob meeting. The younger, more ambitious members of the Sound and Criminal Intelligence Squads knew that he had a wealth of experience and expertise in the field of electronic surveillance, but that he had grown complacent and avoided taking on new responsibilities. He wasn't too popular either with the men who worked for him because of his habit of pissing in the sink at the monitoring plants that he supervised.

Some people will be seized to urinate in the strangest places, I guess. A former Secret Service agent named Rubino told me once he had been assigned to the protection of President Lyndon Baines Johnson. He said that on more than one occasion while the president was staying at his ranch in the Frankericksburg area of Texas, he observed LBJ during early morning hours in his pajamas and bathrobe take a leak off one of the balconies.

When I stopped to think about it, I felt ashamed of my grousing about how insecure our monitoring plant was in the Golden Gate Hotel. We had a spacious suite of rooms as did Carlo on the other side of the wall. The two double beds were comfortable, the air-conditioning worked and the ventilation was good, though we could not utilize the balcony for fear of being seen by Gambino or his visitors. I put this in perspective because the 24/7 accommodations for any monitoring plant can be very problematic.

Such as the one about the situation our agents in New York encountered during the famous Duquesne spy ring investigation. It was the largest espionage case in United States history at the time in 1941 that ended in convictions of thirty three members of a Nazi German espionage network, headed by Frankerick "Fritz" Duquesne. During one of the Bureau's counterintelligence operations, there were two agents on duty in a monitoring plant next to one of the spy's rooms. It was their responsibility to operate a motion picture camera and sound recording system that had been installed on the other side of a one-way mirror. The agents who were manning the plant happened to be heavy smokers. They unknowingly depleted the amount of available oxygen in the room, which affected one of the agents greatly to the point of his collapse.

The field office Supervisor, Jack Danahy, related to me how he received a call for help from the unaffected agent and went to the plant with another to take the incapacitated man to the hospital. This delicate dance had to be accomplished without alerting the spy they were investigating in the adjoining room. They exercised an abundance of caution as they entered the monitoring plant without raising any suspicions. The ailing agent was able to stand, but with support, so they walked him into a bureau car and drove him to the hospital. A medical test there indicated a lack of room oxygen that probably proceeded the epileptic attack the agent had sustained. But then arose the problem of continued medical attention, which demanded an official diagnosis. The attending doctor was placed in a moral dilemma. If the hospital reported what was learned about the agent's medical condition, he would have been forced to resign or been dismissed because of his lack of judgment. Such was the strict nature of Hoover's FBI. The job obviously was important to him because he had a family to support.

Danahy, overseeing the situation and was a decent human being himself, was sympathetic to the problem of representing both the interests of the FBI and also saving the agent's job. Their concerns were obvious to the examining doctor who solved the quandary by volunteering his medical opinion that the agent's physical condition was not permanent and would not be a liability to the FBI long term. The agent was placed on limited duty in the office and continued to contribute in a productive way until his retirement.

Compared to the Duquesne spy case, where an important espionage investigation would have been compromised, the situation that Frank and I found ourselves in with a plush suite next to Carlo was small potatoes, but it did cause concern. It still would have been more secure for us to be sequestered farther away. My proximity to the bug room created a double element of risk for us to be discovered by the Gambinos next door and there was damn good reason for this. The crime lord in particular who we were eavesdropping had seen me previously under circumstances that were certain to have been impressed on his memory, in particular, my face and my name.

It was after the Apalachin fiasco that I was part of a small number of FBI agents who first dogged Carlo Gambino's steps as we poked and prodded into his private business, his personal life and criminal activities. His friends, relatives, business and criminal associates, I was sure, had informed him of who I was after I had paid them all a visit at various times and asked countless questions about him.

Later, when agent James Mulroy took over management of Carlo's investigation after I was transferred off the squad to the Miami office, he was kind enough to give me recognition for the work I had started and expanded with Gambino. I knew then that I had left the investigation in good hands. He was an excellent investigator and at the same time displayed leadership qualities that were rewarded later by his assignment as a supervisor of an OC squad.

During the bugging op, to kill time when we had a spare moment, I filled in Doerner on what I knew about La Cosa Nostra, Carlo Gambino and Tommy Palmer in particular.

FBI Special Agent, Peter C. Clemente (1950-1976)

Apalachin, NY (1957)
The Mob conclave that changed the world

The Apalachin home of Joseph Barbara, where he hosted a meeting of Mafia bosses in 1957.

Joseph "the Barber" Barbara
Apalachin mob host

Carlo Gambino
Unofficial Boss of Bosses and Crime Lord of the world, with largest known gang of psychopaths, killers and thieves

Golden Gate Hotel
Miami Beach, FL (1962)
Historic first ever wiretap of Carlo Gambino

Tommy Greco, AKA Tommy Palmer
Trusted Gambino Lieutenant,
who futilely searched for the bug

Chapter Four
Tommy Palmer, Lion in Decline
*"I don' t fit the FBI mold 100%.
I'm Sicilian on both sides."*

I took great care to avoid being seen by Carlo. I couldn't help thinking that the crime boss was bound to suspect that his room was bugged if he were to come across me in the hallway just as I exited the room next to his suite. I couldn't afford either to bump into Carlo and his crew in the lobby of the hotel. Tommy also knew me from New York. He operated out of Lanza's Italian Restaurant on Second Avenue in Manhattan. It was several years later after the Gambino bugging operation, when I began working in the Miami field office, that I would often spoil his day by showing up where he lived at the Taormina Cooperative Apartments on Ocean Boulevard in the Hallandale-Hollywood area of Broward County.

For what its worth, Tommy Palmer was the only LCN member who ever threatened me to my face. It was an oblique threat in that he said, "Clemente, if I'm the bad guy they say I am, did you ever stop to think I might get so pissed off at you that I might do to you what I am supposed to have done to others? I'm older than you, I'm sick and could croak any day. I have less to lose."

Before I answered him, I studied his face deliberately for several seconds, looking into his eyes. They did not waver, blink, or turn aside. I began by speaking in Sicilian, the language I spoke before I learned English so that I could put more menace and meaning into what I had to say.

I told him, "The thought came to my mind that you and some of your amici (friends) might be so foolish. I know Carlo told his guys that it was closed season on FBI agents, anyone who 'hits' an agent would get whacked. He himself said, 'It would start a war with the FBI that Cosa Nostra was sure to lose.'"

"What you want to remember is that during the war while you and your cummari (comrades) were stealing and selling gas ration coupons and stolen meat on the black market or killing one another, most of the FBI agents my age were killing enemy soldiers wholesale.

"You think they got us reined in by the law? Just like I can't rely on you obeying Gambino's rule against hitting agents, don't make the mistake of thinking FBI rules are going to handcuff me. I don't fit the FBI mold 100%. I'm Sicilian on both sides. Besides, there's a strain of insanity in my family the Bureau did not pick up on. My mother told me when she learned I was investigating you SOB's, if anything happened to me, she wouldn't stop with the guy who did it, but would kill all the products of his seed. That's the Sicilian in her talking, pure vendetta. There is no mafia blood in my family. Her family in the old country were victims of your self-styled 'Men of Honor' who were actually 'Men of Dishonor.'

"Now, I'm not counting on my mother doing what I can do myself. You ought to start worrying that I might take your veiled threat seriously and launch a preemptive strike of my own. My motto is, shoot first, then ask questions.

"If you have any intention of killing me, Tommy, you had better do it here and now. Because if I leave here convinced you mean to have me killed, I'll look for the soonest opportunity to put your lights out. In the meantime, should something happen to me, be advised that the top red flagged serial in your case file will be the memorandum I will prepare today as soon as I get to the office saying that you made a veiled threat on my life. You will be suspect number one and if you are so annoyed by my occasional visit to your condominium to see if you are dead or alive, just think what it will be like when they come down on you like a ton of bricks. Then again, you and your kin might have to deal with my mother. She will not have to be convinced beyond a reasonable doubt of your guilt like a jury would."

I waited for Tommy to clarify his intentions.

Tommy Palmer smiled a tired smile. It was really a shadow of a smile, not a vigorous, robust one, like that from a happy, healthy man. "Your mother sounds like my mother," he said, "God rest her soul. She used similar words once when I was having a problem with a guy, a partner of mine. I didn't say I was going to do anything. I said, suppose… suppose is pure speculation. Hey, I like you, even though you're a pest and cramp my style around here. It was no different in New York, no… I take that back, you were worse in New York. You think I like you coming here reminding my neighbors that the FBI is interested in me? They look at me like I'm public enemy number one. I'm a gambler, not a young punk trying to make his bones. Let's both back off and call a truce."

I told him I would tell my troops to stand down, but not to stack their guns. He really looked ill so I told him to check his blood sugar because he had previously mentioned that it was very high. He sold his apartment not long after and returned to live full time in New York. If my memory serves me, he had a house in Long Beach.

I didn't feel even a little shame for landing on him with both feet. It was agent Joe Melenky in the New York office, our premier undercover agent on the Criminal Squad in the Fifties and Sixties who told me that in criminal cases, the Bureau's usual "Dominate the Situation" advice translates to "be firm, aggressive and menacing."

In the case of Tommy Palmer, we had a sick, perhaps depressed Mafioso stoking the fires of his manhood by intimating that he might off an agent if the mood struck him. I knew from the length of time he had been in Cosa Nostra that he was initiated into the brotherhood at a time when participation in a murder was mandatory for all recruits. Did he mean to commit suicide by killing an agent? I didn't really think so. Or was he killing time and amusing himself by suggesting he might react in a violent manner to the irritating FBI checks on his activities while staying at his winter home? Maybe, but the facts didn't warrant a killing.

It wouldn't take much physical strength for Tommy to let out a contract of murder. Gambino, his boss, at age 71 in 1973, while suffering from a severe and debilitating cardiac disease, effortlessly sent out the word to his underboss Aniello Dellacroce to put the final screws on James McBratney, the suspected kidnapper and murderer of his nephew Manny Gambino.

When I first encountered Palmer in New York, he had what he called sugar diabetes, so I boned up on as much medical information about it as I could to use it as a conversation starter in the hope I could get him talking about a more relevant life-threatening subject like La Cosa Nostra. Since I did not have the threat of a long stretch of years in prison to hang over his head, my efforts to turn him into an informant never saw the light of day. He was probably sick and tired of my efforts to get intel out of him and hoped to scare me off with his threat. It had all started when I was in the New York office when he was a younger, healthier man and now here I was manning an audio tap on his boss, Carlo whom he was visiting on a regular basis in sunny Florida.

When the operation concluded after six long weeks, whenever I passed the Taormina Apartments or the Golden Gate Hotel, I thought of Tommy Palmer and the fits he gave us looking for the audio bug.

Chapter Five
The Summit Of Mount Apalachin
A Horde Of Actors From Central Casting About To Film "Little Caesar."

It would be hard to say if I would have been on the other side of Gambino's wall if the big mob conclave had not materialized. But its momentous occurrence did create an epic sea change in organized crime history and probably in the criminal empire of Carlo Gambino, mostly in his favor.

It would be accurate to describe the doomed Apalachin fiasco on November 14, 1957, which Gambino was an important part of, as a National Convention meeting of the upper level of leadership of La Cosa Nostra. In the aftermath, while on the FBI's Top Hoodlum Squad, I was the first ever to write an official government summary report on Gambino and his past. What we eventually came to learn was that New York mob boss, Vito Genovese not only was responsible for the selection of the gathering site of hoodlums, but was also a participant in events that made the meeting necessary. Gambino was a large part of the reason, who needed to discuss his ascension to Albert Anastasia's throne after the madman from Murder Incorporated was butchered in his barber chair. Gambino, it seemed, had taken over Albert's crime family, but not until after it had swollen to an alarming size, made possible by the unauthorized "sale" of memberships for around $25,000 a clip.

After the horrible discovery of the meeting by the New York State Police, Vito came in for sharp criticism for bullying his associates into utilizing the estate of Joseph Barbara as a meeting place. His home, with a large number of acres, was in a largely rural setting adjacent to a small town. The influx of over 100 mobsters of obvious similar ethnic origin, wearing Italian custom-tailored suits and Italian shoes and driving expensive Cadillacs, Lincolns and Mercedes was bound to draw attention. Barbara's arrangement with local motels for a large number of rooms to be reserved for November 14th and his servant's purchase in town of large quantities of choice steaks, Italian sausage, expensive liquor and cigars did not go unnoticed.

They would have been better advised to book a convention site in a major metropolitan area than meet on the estate of a former bootlegger and suspect in three murder investigations. Barbara was also an object of special interest to New York State Police Sgt. Edgar Croswell, whose informants in town alerted him to the arrival of what looked a horde of actors from Central Casting about to film "Little Caesar." Croswell during the investigation of a bad-check case, spotted Barbara's son making room reservations for a large number of visitors and later received word from a butcher that an order had been placed for 200-pounds of steak and other meat products to be delivered to Barbara's mansion.

The suppliers of other gourmet delicacies reported to Croswell, purchases of expensive food sufficient to feed a small army, all billed to, paid for and picked up by one of Joseph Barbara employees. The fact that bootlegger Barbara had invested his profits from criminal activities in the purchase of a Canada Dry Bottling and Distributing franchise, in Croswell's eyes, didn't make Joe a legitimate businessman. He knew that Barbara was diverting some of the sugar he purchased, normally to be used in manufacturing soda pop, into the production of illicit alcohol. John Ruston, an agent with the Alcohol and Tobacco Tax division of the Treasury Department was working with Croswell in an investigation of Barbara, an apparent former bootlegger, despite his cloak of respectability, who had never put rum running behind him.

Croswell had seen enough of the suspicious characters with the shark skin suits invading his territory. Assisted by another trooper and two agents from the United States Treasury, roadblocks were set up at the edge of Barbara's estate to haul in a catch of big bad barracuda. One of Barbara's men, returning from an errand, noticed the unusual collection of cops and blew the whistle on something that proved to be both comical and historical. Over one hundred of the country's top Mafia chieftains panicked at the news of a potential bust, knowing full well that if the authorities found out about their conspiracy to organize the largest meeting they ever had, all hell would break loose.

The flight began. Men who probably hadn't run a lick since galloping down the street years before when running bookie numbers, started huffing and puffing out of the compound in every direction. Like headless chickens they ran for the woods, soiling their high-priced Italian loafers and fine cut clothes. Eventually, 60 of them were caught—scared, embarrassed and humiliated at having been chased like ordinary dogs through the rough countryside. Some were stopped at road blocks in their showy limousines like Gambino and a few others, including the steely Sam "Momo" Giancana from Chicago, decided to stay put in Barbara's house, realizing that escape was a ludicrous option.

Croswell and the State Police notified the FBI immediately after the roundup and told anybody who would listen that some high-profile hoods had been held for questioning. Actually, there was no legal cause for the authorities to hold these men in the first place and a subsequent charge of obstruction of justice was later dismissed in 1960 for insufficient evidence of a conspiracy. During the roundup, Barbara's reluctant guests were questioned about the purpose of their visit while police counted a grand total of $300,000 in cash lifted from their pockets, along with identification. Of course, these "honorable" men were only there to see their "old pal, Joe" who recently announced that he had developed a heart condition of sorts. "Sure," the cops smirked as they searched the men further, recording and photographing each of Barbara's guests with the intent to put the finger on them.

It might not be too fanciful to say that Genovese had moved the entire upper echelon of LCN leadership under the microscopic lens of law enforcement that pivotal day. The Southern Confederacy during the Civil War had its Gettysburg moment as a turning point, which led to its defeat, and La Cosa Nostra's Gettysburg was the Apalachin conclave of November 14, 1957. But the long, demanding battle against this group of organized criminals would continue through the years with the agents who followed in our footsteps, all but wiping it out.

Not long after the big Summit crashed and burned, I was given a thick file with photographs of each conspirator, along with a dossier enumerating their involvement at Barbara's compound and where they were located at the time of their arrest. Also included was an up-to-date sheet of every criminal activity they had all been charged with. There were some heavy hitters involved and as I leafed through the countless faces, it was like a high school year book album gone bad.

Very few of these short, squat men looked anywhere near dashing or had any glamorized Hollywood mobster looks. Some had that working class meat and potatoes appearance like Joseph "Joe Rivers" Scalise. Others, like Paul Vario and Guido Penosi, resembled grade school dropouts who couldn't hold a job to save their lives. Then there were those like Ralph LaPanzina and Carlo Gambino who had a sort of grandfatherly facade that caught you off guard at first. Paternal or not, Mr. Gambino's hawk-like eyes stared back at me from the mug shot I was studying during the writing of my summary.

At that moment, I decided to pay him a little visit.

Chapter Six
Boss of Bosses, Destroyer of Worlds
"I have nothing to say to you."

During the long hours I spend eavesdropping on him, I sat quietly in my chair with only a faint hum of the tape recorder coming through the headset. There was sort of a blind man's need to place a face with the voice I heard continuously through the wall, so as I listened and my partner's audio tape wound through the spool, I thought about the first time I saw Gambino's notorious eyes in a mug shot, as well as the surprise chance meeting we had.

I distinctly remember it was a cloudy autumn day in Brooklyn, with a bit of a chill that sort of hung on me as I waited in my car on the street where Mr. Gambino lived. As was my modus operandi for many years, I preferred more often than not to approach a wiseguy at an opportune time by myself, without a partner. It was just common sense. If you approach a known criminal alone, in search of information from them, they tend to be a little less apprehensive. If you were a street hood, would you feel more inclined to have your antenna up when approached by two or more FBI agents? Your chances of gathering any pertinent intel plummets to about zero. Then again, there were risks involved when interviewing any of these characters mano a mano without a backup. It was written in stone that all of these unsavory marauders had killed others to "make their bones" to begin with, and more than a few had a screw or two loose in their sociopathic profiles. Even though I had been "mobbed up" myself with the Bureau at my back, do you really trust completely whether one of these killers was having a bad day or not to choose turning you into nothing more than a grease spot? With Gambino, however, those thoughts hadn't entered my mind. I trusted him enough not to do anything nonsensical.

Gambino's house was an upper middle-class home with a high front stoop. I knew he would be leaving during morning hours for his usual business schedule and it was my plan to accost him as he walked to his car. I saw him give his wife Kate a kiss at the door when he left the house. Kate would later accompany him to the Golden Gate, when I listened in on her husband. While in the next room, Carlo would politely ask his wife to iron a shirt for him or conduct other small favors like any couple would do. There were no arguments and the marriage was a give-and-take on both sides. Kate Gambino knew exactly what she was getting into when she tied the knot with Carlo many years before. The two of them were first cousins with Kate originating from a family of hoodlums previously. Her brother, Paul Castellano was a powerful wiseguy and after Carlo's death, his ascension as the Gambino family boss was immediate. Kate had all the training. She was a dutiful Mafia wife who respected and honored her husband while keeping her mouth shut and asking no questions during the 14-karat ride her life. She and her Carlo had several children, one of her daughters marrying a doctor and one of their sons, Joseph eventually carrying on the family name as a manipulator of New York's garment trucking business.

As Gambino headed in my direction, there were no associates flanking him as he usually had during working hours at this stage of his career and there was no glare of the public spotlight that came to be. He was also secure in his stature as the capo of New York's largest family, and any apprehension of danger this early in the morning was a minor consideration. Mr. Gambino, as always, was properly dressed, never looking like some of the dandies that felt the urge to make a name for themselves through their clothes. He was wearing his usual, long, gray, Chesterfield coat and snap brim hat that day and the sharp, carved nose set against those dark, penetrating eyes bored into his face, prominently led the way.

I was far from being nervous at the time and nothing in my mind threatened to have me say or do anything that was unprofessional or foolish. I wasn't a rookie agent by any means and my years of experience with interviewing bad characters of different hues made me jaded enough to want to probe this man that was fast making a legend for himself. After Apalachin, Gambino had been assigned to me as one of the organized crime subjects I needed to study and build a file on. It was my responsibility to develop his background and associates, employment history, arrest records, contacts with other police agencies, fingerprint records, and anything else I could uncover.

On that particular day, I wanted only two things. There was scant opportunity that I would even think about arresting such a well-buffered uber criminal in the first place, which was irrational and without legal justification. Unless, however, he physically attacked me with intent to do harm to a federal agent. But that was also less of a chance than winning the lottery even after buying up all the tickets. One goal in mind was to get a rise out of him, and second, to study his voice. To my knowledge, up to that point, no other agent had spoken personally with him face to face. What sort of temperament he had also interested me. If I could determine whether he was easily irritated or even spooked by my presence, it would help in the personal profile I would put together on him.

Even the sound of his voice as I talked to him would come in handy down the road if someone needed to identify him during any kind of surveillance activity. So far, what little of Mr. Gambino that was known was his dubious past as a bootlegger in the '20s, his known criminal association as head of the Anastasia family and a suspect employment history as the head of SGS Associates, a labor relations company.

Still, as he walked toward me, I knew this wasn't chopped liver I was dealing with. I didn't pay attention to the two bodyguards that stepped out of his car to drive him off. I knew that they saw me immediately and ignored them and their concerns that I might be a possible gunman as I flashed my credentials at Gambino once I got close to him. I purposely stood in his path to the car door so that he would stop and fix his eyes on my badge. I spoke as calmly as possible in Sicilian, the tongue I had first learned as a child.

"Mr. Gambino," I said, "My name is Peter Clemente, I'm with the FBI. There are a few things I'd like to ask you, if you have a moment."

Under the hat, his eyes moved from my badge directly up to me. He was small framed like I knew he would be and not very physically imposing. Like many a mobster with an Italian background, he was rather short. Little men, most of them, but very dangerous. There were of course the occasional Luca Brasi types who were tall and powerful, but with a gun, knife or rope, the short could be as deadly. But Gambino's eyes more than made up for it. The hawk was sizing me up and like a bird of prey zeroing in on a tasty meal from hundreds of yards above. Gambino seemed to swoop down and then reject me for a dinner that he would give anything to have otherwise. For the short beat in which he waited to say something, there was little emotion in his face, save for a look of disgust.

Ultimately, when Gambino died in bed in 1976, looking much like he had during most of his adult years after surviving open-heart surgery and loss of weight, the passage of time accentuated his big ears, droopy eyelids, red-rimmed brown eyes and hawk nose. More casual unforgiving observers wanted to call it a banana nose. But victims of his malignant look, who had heard either spoken or unspoken threats from him, thought it resembled the beak of a hungry raptor instead.

A legitimate businessman and partner of Gambino, (from 1945-1954 with Bell Paper and Bag company), once told me how one malevolent look from the crime lord had him quaking in his shoes. The Boss fixed his withering look on the man when he told Gambino he wanted to end their business relationship. Gambino, as secretary-treasurer of the firm, was receiving the lion's share of the profits without doing a lick of work. I was struck at the time by the depth and extent of fear the businessman said engulfed him, similar to King Hamlet's ghost, "each particular hair to stand on end, like quills upon the fretful porcupine. "

A book, authored by two FBI agents, *Boss of Bosses*, both not being of Italian ancestry and tending to stereotype Italians as either organ grinders or fruit and vegetable hawkers, claimed that, "Gambino has been described as resembling a fruit peddler and the characterization is apt. One could imagine the old man in front of a cart full of apples bending down slowly, painfully to hand a Golden Delicious to a little girl while pinching her cheek and inquiring about her behavior in school."

Not quite. Anyone who encountered Carlo the same as I had ever said he looked like a fruit peddler. It was never more evident in my meeting with him that chilly morning as I looked into his eyes.

"I have nothing to say to you," Gambino said flatly. His voice was deep and guttural.

The fact that I spoke Sicilian didn't seem to surprise him, possibly because he had heard about me from the other wiseguys under his watch. I was a little conspicuous in that I was a rare agent at the time that could speak the dialect, which was somewhat different than the language of mainland Italian.

"It won't take but a minute or two of your time," I said just as evenly.

"What could you possibly want that's of interest? I'm just a business man."

"Well, that may be, but you have some business dealings that I find interesting."

I could see that annoyed him. Mission accomplished for one of my goals. "I said I'm a business man, an honest businessman. I see you're Sicilian also. You're one of us. Why are you bothering me?"

"I'd like to ask you about one of your associates at SGS, to get a timeframe on when the two of you were supposed to have had a meeting together."

Gambino was whip smart and knew that I was just trying to break his balls for whatever reason. He didn't like it all and it tipped him over the edge ever so slightly.

"I told you I have nothing to say to you. You say you're with the FBI, but you're nothing but a *sbirro* (police spy) like in the old country. You should be ashamed of yourself."

He wanted me to come down to his emotional level, but I wouldn't follow his cue. I kept what I had to say as calm and collected as I could, doing it the shrewd Sicilian way. "I should be ashamed? The only one who should be ashamed is yourself, Mr. Gambino. Number one, for the criminal activity you've been involved with for the longest time that's been no secret. Number two, for the amount of shame you've given to the large majority of Italian Americans who came to this country, like my parents, intending to do things the honest way. No, sir. The shame is all yours."

Gambino lowered his eyes to stare at me. There was a combination of respect fused with anger smoldering through him. All he could reply was a quick profanity, "*vaffanculo*," in Sicilian as he wheeled past me for his car. The bodyguards, none too happy with me either, could only open his door to drive him off instead of beating me into the ground.

Mission accomplished on both fronts, I was satisfied with what I came for. Carlo Gambino, Boss of Bosses, Crime Lord of the World now knew more than ever that he was a little less anonymous than he cared to be. Would he then later share me at the dinner table when breaking bread with Kate while sipping some vino? If he did, it would have been through an annoyed remark about someone that showed him disrespect that morning, making me look as small as possible to his wife.

Or, quite possibly, after the dishes were cleared and they prepared for bed, would he be plotting under his breath to sign my death warrant? Only God and Carlo knew. But God the Father was also aware that Gambino was the lion king of the largest assemblage of member career criminals, numbering in the hundreds, who each in turn held sway over a core of criminal associates of their own, ready to kill for Don Carlo without question. Many of them hoped, even prayed for induction into his ranks. How much further up the ladder could anyone go than with raw, naked power, altering him into "a destroyer of worlds," as from the Hindu sacred text, Bhagavad Gita. It was the kind of power that could send men to their graves with just a nod of the head or even one of those looks that his business partner had talked to me about.

There were too many striking characteristics about this man that kept tugging at me from literature. In someways, Mr. Gambino reminded me both of Faust and Mephistopheles rolled into one. Faust, the alchemist because Gambino was also a bootlegger who distilled alcohol and who sold his soul to the devil in exchange for power, worldly possessions and experience. He could also pass for the devil, Mephistopheles within the legend, to whom Faust sold his soul to. He was Faust when he was recruited and took the blood oath, renouncing God and the government, and Mephistopheles when he administered the oath himself to recruits of his family who traded their souls to him.

As much as the darkness shrouded him, it was captivating to peel back the layers of Gambino knowing that he was still part of the human condition, tragic flaws, warts and all.

Chapter Seven
Moment of Judgement
"We need to pull the wire, Pete."

A few years later, at the Golden Gate, while I listened in on him, I came to appreciate the subject I was studying as being more than just an object to stalk. I became a hunter who comes to appreciate the prowess of the animal he learns to respect from afar. I knew how Mr. Gambino played the cat and mouse game. There were a few conspiratorial conversations if any that we recorded in those six weeks. Gambino was extremely discreet, never blurting anything out while conducting meetings with some of his associates, usually with Tommy Luchese (aka, Three Finger Brown, because of a few missing digits) or on the phone. If there was something to talk about, he had enough sense to turn up the volume on the TV or wander out to the balcony with whoever he was with so that the noise of the nearby ocean surf would drown out the discussions.

During one of those long periods, I mentioned to Frank how Carlo had traveled to the Apalachin meeting in 1957 with his brother-in-law/first cousin, Paul Castellano and Armando Rava, a soldier in his family. A few years after the trip to upstate New York, Carlo had not allowed a lifetime association and friendship stand in the way of his ordering hitmen to make Rava disappear. Rava apparently never got over the murder of his favorite boss, Albert Anastasia, nor his disappointment over the failure of Aniello

Dellacroce to claim his rightful role as boss. Aniello was happy with half a loaf and lived. Rava carped, complained and plotted, and then disappeared into the great unknown where Judge Carter had disappeared.

I told Frank to stop and think about it. If the old man could have had Rava clipped, imagine what he could have done to a couple of strangers like us. He knew I was pulling his chain. "Yeah, right. You know as well as I do that it's closed season on FBI agents. But the way you look though and the way you're able to talk to talk and walk the walk, they might mistake you for one of them."

He was right about that, but only in the way that I resembled them as another Sicilian. Over Frank's shoulder, we had the TV turned on, but always with the sound off. It was showing the Eddie G. Robinson gangster film, *Key Largo*, which was set not too far from us down the road in Key West. How dissimilar though was Robinson, who looked like a preening Hollywood gangster compared to the flesh and blood Mafia chieftain who was no more than a few feet from us in the next suite.

I continued the microphone surveillance and from what I could hear, Tommy Palmer and Jimmy Dee were still firing off their venom laced Sicilian. The furniture was still being moved around, but not as frantically or abruptly as before. The hunt was not slacking off, but was transferred to the lighting appliances, the floor and underneath the bed.

"Damn it, Tommy," I heard, "what kind of a dump is this? There's dead roaches under here, spiders and...arggh! It's a f--king used rubber (condom)! Geez, marone!"

"Check the lamp," said Palmer.

"I'm washing my hands first," said Jimmy. "Crap almighty. Where am I supposed to look? What the f--k do they look like anyway?"

"Maybe it looks like a f--kin' olive, who knows. I'm in the dentist office with a Newsweek and I'm readin' that the CIA has a bug that looks like an olive and they can put the damn thing in a martini glass. You believe this?"

The story strikes Carlo as funny. He has switched on the TV to watch a news program and obviously is not participating in the fruitless search for the bug. Carlo laughs and asks Tommy, "Did they say anything in the story, what would happen if somebody swallowed the olive?"

Tommy said, "The CIA agent who wanted to hear what someone at another table was saying, would order a martini with no olive. When it was served to him, he would slip his olive bug in the drink and the bug acted like a small radio transmitter so it would pick up and send out the conversation at the next table."

"Marone," Carlo laughed, "no wonder our taxes are so high. If this guy's olive can pick up what's being said at the next table, he should be able to hear with his own two ears what they're saying."

Tommy lets the conversation die after not disputing his leader's wisdom. "You're right, boss."

"They can put one of those things anywhere they want to," said Jimmy. "You're wasting your time. Like I keep saying, those bastards could be down the street, in the next room or in your car for all we know."

I had difficulty hearing what continued because Carlo raises the volume on the TV and the news anchor is coming in loud and clear. I have to guess what the bug hunters are up to.

I hear the night table being jostled around the bed and then there was a loud shriek, followed by some stomping sounds. I knew it couldn't be that they found the bug because the A-block was located right behind the night table. Carlo snaps off the TV and I hear Tommy, the head bug hunter say, "When I reached under the night table, there was a brown recluse spider that ran out."

Carlo was none too pleased, but not about his health. "Tommy, you stomped the sucker right into the carpet. What a mess!"

"You know that spider could've killed you, what with your diabetes and your age. "

I updated Frank, who was getting more concerned with the situation as I relayed it to him.

Finally, he had enough. "Let's pull the wire, Pete."

"I don't think it's a good idea to unplug it," I said firmly.

"Well, we have to do something," he said. "They keep crawling all over each other just to find the damn thing."

"Look, if you pull the wire, there's a more than a remote chance they'll hear the disturbance. Like maybe a crackling or something. Who knows. Then they'll really know where to look."

"Maybe you're right. I wouldn't want to clue them where to look. Let's move the bed anyway so if we plan to pull it we won't waste time."

I could see that Frank's Teutonic nature didn't allow for expressions of emotion and he was battling to keep in his fear of being unjustly blamed for a possible audio tap discovery. We eventually came to the agreement that it would be better if we sat tight and kept our voices down. It was definitely a tense moment. Gambino and his crew were on one side of the wall, scouring through every part of their room looking for the plant, while Frank and I were on our side, crawling out of our skins. The tension was wearing me thin, too. I had been manning the headset without a break because the three men were speaking only Sicilian, which of course was foolish. They should've realized the FBI has Sicilian speaking agents on their payroll, although not many.

Then, out of the blue, a final determination arose from the fog of war. I sensed what was about to happen. "Wait," I told him, holding up my hand like Moses about to deliver the eleventh commandment.

Frank abruptly stopped pacing on the rug to face me for the longest time as he waited. "Well, what is it?"

"Apparently, it's time for Carlo's nap," I smiled. "He told them to clean up the mess they made looking for the tap and said, 'You're wasting my time. Clean up and get out of here before Kate comes back with Kitty (Luchese).' That's it."

To say that Frank looked pleased with the outcome was an understatement. He slumped back on the couch, shook his head and smiled. "If you weren't here to translate all that Sicilian, I wouldn't have had any idea they were looking for it."

I grinned. "The way things turned out, you would have been better off not knowing they suspected it and were actually looking for it."

"That's right. I almost creamed my drawers when you told me they were hunting for it. I suppose we wait for Tommy and Jimmy to clear out before we go eat." Frank was getting some good home-cooked meals at his mother-in-law's place in Homestead down the road, while I frequented the Polly Davis cafeteria a lot. The strain of the moment had lifted from him and while he turned away, I let out a sigh of relief, not just for myself, but the anxiety that Frank had been going through.

The thunderclouds were gone. I was grateful for the momentary reprieve, but what if they had discovered the plant? Would they immediately know there was somebody or a group of people nearby absorbing every syllable that Carlo uttered? Would they instantly burst in from the next room with blood in their eyes and guns blazing for violating their right to secrecy? Exactly what would have gone through their minds? I had to analyze it professionally.

In all likelihood, nothing would've happened. If I had an accurate read at all on Gambino, he most likely would have followed a time-honored Sicilian credo, *never let your enemies know of your anger*. To do otherwise would have let them know that they had gotten under your skin. Mr. Gambino, even if he did smolder under such a circumstance, was always smart enough to not let his poker hand show. His men would do the grumbling for him, talking loud enough so we could hear the insults about what degenerates we were maybe or how we didn't earn enough to support our families, prostituting ourselves as gutless police spies to make a buck. And then, as loudly as they rumbled in like the rain clouds, they would quietly pack up, check out and catch the next bird back to New York.

At the end of a typical day, after Gambino's guests left in the late evening, some lines I felt had to be drawn. As much as a dangerous man Gambino was to the economic climate of the United States, I still had respect for his private affairs. When it was time for lovemaking and Carlo and his wife needed privacy like any every other married couple, that's when I felt business for the day was over. There was no need for further intrusion and nobody at Bureau headquarters would have argued there were any further noteworthy discoveries to be made while the two had conjugal relations. No one ordered me to do so, but some things are just more common sense than others. When those times came, the reel-to-reel stopped in mid-turn and didn't resume again until morning.

Whenever it was time to get out and take a break, I took advantage of it by dropping a few sedentary pounds that needed attention. Down the road on North Miami Beach was the Blue Seas Motel. They had terrific broiled mackerel there and my steady diet of it over several weeks did the trick for my weight. But as much as I wanted to escape the confines of my jail cell-like set up at the motel to get some fresh tropical air for a change, it wasn't to be. Work followed me there, too.

Like a steady run of barracuda that made their way down the Atlantic stream, I ran into more than a few wiseguys I recognized from up in New York. Most of them were there on business and pleasure. It was the winter season and the place for northerners to thaw out at the time was sunny Miami Beach, where the neighborhood boys migrated, too. At the time, Miami was considered an open market for crime opportunity. No particular family ruled the roost there and wasn't allowed to. So, when I looked up from my plate of mackerel from time to time, it wasn't unusual to spot the unsavory likes of several mobsters I might have previously talked to in New York just a few short weeks ago. The only difference being a wardrobe on some of them that could be described as comical. Straw hats, very dark sunglasses and loud Bermuda shirts were the "norm" and sometimes I couldn't help thinking it would be nice if they all dressed like that up north so they would be a lot easier to spot.

My instinct to collect new data on them for their bulging files was a temptation. Some of these hoodlums were high profile with big connections, while others were just scratching out a living, working for other wiseguys and doing their bid. The idea to talk to a few of them didn't last long though. My sole job was to watch Mr. Gambino closely, and after slipping out of the motel and making sure he didn't see or possibly recognize me from a few years ago, I also made sure there wouldn't be others running into me to pass the word along that I was around. Word about me in Miami Beach might have set off a connection between Mr. Gambino's visit and mine to South Florida. Luckily, no one ever connected the dots and everything stayed calm as far as the mob boss and his associates were concerned.

After the bugging search episode ended with the hoods, Frank tossed me the keys to his pride and joy, a 1957 Pontiac station wagon, wood paneling and all, and said, "Here you go, paisano, you earned it."

I drove down for the usual Polly Davis and then at the end of the day, I walked back to the motel, thinking about my family waiting for me at home and missing them as much as anybody could. The sun was going down into the Atlantic and the breeze from the 72-degree day lingered on my face as I watched dusk arrive. I thought about how Carlo Gambino and I, with a similar ethnic background, shared the same line of work, but to different ends. We both had secrets to tell. It was information that could disrupt lives, change fortunes or alter the course of coming events, depending on whose hands it fell into. It was no secret either that the two of us shared pressing family matters back home—his much more infamous and deadly than mine.

About The Authors

Peter C. Clemente was a veteran Special Agent of the Federal Bureau of Investigation from 1950-1976.
As a part of the Greatest Generation, he was reared in the Great Depression following his birth in Brooklyn, NY, in 1922, the second son of Sicilian immigrants who embarked upon America through the gates of Ellis Island with little in their pockets. Their adoring son was not dissuaded with the lack of money in the family coffers and always made lemonade from lemons by keeping his trousers freshly pressed under the mattress of his bed for the next school day until he was voted Best Dressed in his senior high school class. However, a couple of years previous, something was featured at a local movie theater that would change his life. It was Jimmy Cagney starring in G-MAN that made him swear that fighting crime was going to be his "crusade," when the time came. World War II came knocking on his door eventually and following his service as a surgical Army tech in the Philippines, the GI Bill was used to put him through law school at St. Johns before soon hanging his shingle as an attorney in the Big Apple. His "crusade" came looking for him when a cousin expressed concern that Peter was thinking of applying for a new career with the FBI and was warned, "Forget it, Pete. They don't take Italians." Clemente indignantly set out to prove the Bureau wrong and soon found himself being interviewed across the desk of an agent with a very obvious Italian

name, which immediately demolished any notions of discrimination and soon led to training at the FBI Academy in Quantico, VA and then a welcoming handshake from J. Edgar Hoover himself. It wasn't until a few years later, while in the New York field office performing internal security background checks for individuals applying for a sensitive government positions that special agent Clemente heard some national news that would take his life on another course. Following the infamous Mafia conclave in upstate New York, in 1957, where every powerful mobster in U.S. history met in clandestine fashion, Clemente immediately put in his request to be a part of the Top Hoodlum Program that Hoover was assembling nationally. As part of the Top Hoodlum Squad in New York, Clemente would soon pen the first ever government summaries written up about notorious gangsters Carlo Gambino and Meyer Lansky. It was after Clemente finished his reports that the inspiration to conduct a never attempted face-to-face interview with Gambino, the Boss of Bosses, on the streets of Brooklyn surfaced. Later, in 1962, the two would cross paths again with Clemente having the honor of listening in on the wiretapped conversations of Gambino and his lieutenants in the next room of his suite at the Golden Gate Hotel in Miami Beach, Florida. These are among some of the notable achievements Clemente carved out, including his close involvement with deciphering historic information from Joe Valachi, the most notorious mob stool pigeon ever. Clemente eventually transferred to the Miami FBI office in 1963 where he continued his organized crime and Mafia battles before retiring in 1976. Still having a bug for the law, he proceeded to pass the Florida bar on his first try and ironically became a criminal defense attorney. The dogged lawman passed away in 2017, still sharp as a tack and just short of his 95th birthday, leaving behind his beautiful wife, Theresa and six adoring children who are still amazed at his legacy of achievements as one of the country's Greatest Generation.

The apple didn't fall far from the tree for Peter's son, co-author G. P. (Gary) Clemente, who spent his boyhood happily in the suburbs of Bergenfield, New Jersey on the other side of New York City's Hudson River during the 50's. When his father transferred to the Miami FBI office in 1963 from the New York Top Hoodlum Squad, he spent his adolescence in

Florida while dearly missing the snow and warm memories of seasonal changes from up North. After graduating from the University of Florida, degreed with a Bachelors in Broadcasting, and after working at a small radio station as a copywriter, he decided to go his own way rather than puddle jump from market to market in search of media communications advancement. The sledding wasn't easy searching for his own path as his tried his hand in television, marketing and advertising, sales and copywriting, freelance work as a journalist with the Dallas Morning News and then Dallas-Fort Worth Independent Newspapers. It was the everyday grind of writing news copy that disciplined him, but then eventually his placement at the old MGM film studios in Culver City, California freed him to creatively craft television scripts and screenplays. While struggling to make his mark in an entertainment business that was unforgiving, he penned and published a children's book that made him the proudest, Cosmo Gets An Ear, about a quirky little boy grappling with the introduction of his first hearing aid, most of which came from the author's own real life experiences. These days, he's still active as a freelance writer in various modes while involved with UNTOLD MAFIA TALES speaking engagements and podcasts about his father and the historic battles between the FBI and the American Mafia's golden years of organized crime from 1950 to its crashing fall in the late 1980s.

www.ingramcontent.com/pod-product-compliance
Lightning Source LLC
Chambersburg PA
CBHW020522030426
42337CB00011B/514